GW01003245

Everyone Wants a Slice...

But Make Sure There's Something Left

by
Johnnie Black

ISBN: 1497320143
ISBN 13: 9781497320147

To my girls:

Sharon, Beth, Jodie, and Connie—all heaven-sent. You enrich my life and bring joy to my heart. Sharon, my wife, friend, and soul mate, you have lived through this with me—thanks for helping me to keep it real.

In memory of Gerald A Titmus. When the light at the end of the tunnel is a train…

Contents

Chapter

Preface

Stressed...But Not Out!

It seems to me that today stress is blamed for everything. It is one of the most overused and misunderstood words. But stress is real, and more and more people are becoming so "stressed out" that it is having a major toll on their health, their families, and almost every area of their lives.

Those who know me might think, "What does he know about stress? He's so laid back, he doesn't do stress." Ask my wife— she has been there in the busyness and when I've cried out in exasperation, "I'm getting sick of this; everybody wants a slice!"

What follows isn't just a dusty theory but what I've learnt and hopefully tried to live over many years. During that time I've juggled and struggled with the pressures of heading up the UK risk management division of what was, at the time, one of Europe's best performing banks, being a management consultant to more than ten companies at board level, being a father of three beautiful girls, being a husband, being a church elder, and being a leader of my church youth work. In my spare time I like to…sleep!

This book isn't about taking all the stress out of your life; that's not realistic, and I don't believe that it is God's way either. I believe there is a certain amount of stress or pressure that is positive. It's about how to manage stress in your life so that you can be stressed but not stressed out. So this book is for all who know what it feels like to be stressed and to scream out, "I'm sick of this; everyone wants a slice!"

A Little Bit About Me

I try to live by the Joseph principal. In Genesis we continually read that people and places were blessed by Joseph's presence. While Joseph was in Potiphar's house, it was blessed; while he was in prison, it was blessed. Ultimately Egypt, as a country in the midst of a famine, was blessed by his presence. As the famine impacted the region, surrounding countries were able to come and buy food, and they were blessed. It should be our desire that wherever we are, it is a better place because of our presence, not by any great qualities that we possess, but by being what the Bible describes in Matthew 5:14 as being the "light of the world."

For example, my father worked in the car repair business. Growing up I loved to go with him to get parts for the cars he was fixing. Sad as it may sound, one of my favourite places was going to the breakers yard—the graveyard of old and damaged cars where we would sometimes find the obscure part that we needed. Given the nature of a breakers yard, it should come as no surprise to you that it can be very coarse and "earthy." I can remember arriving one day and passing the side of the Portakabin office and hearing lots of loud laughter and chat. I also heard someone mention my father's name, and when we reached the door, all the laughter had stopped. Now, I'm not saying that being salt and light of the earth means stopping people from laughing (my dad enjoys joking too…maybe too much), but for the few minutes that we were in the Portakabin, my Dad was salt and light, the conversation was better, and the environment was purified. This stuck with me, so when I commenced my working life, I prayed that no matter how hard it would be (and it was and is hard), I would first and foremostly try to be salt and light. We need to make sure that God is our foundation, the most important thing to us. His objectives for our lives need to come first. If we miss that, we can't expect Him to help us through the busyness.

I believe that there are more than enough "Christian self-help" books already, and I really don't want to add to them unnecessarily, so I hope I haven't.

Please take time to read the Bible passages I refer to, as they will speak more to you than I can. As I have said, what follows are my own experiences of living a busy, "stressful" life!

So here it is.

Johnnie

1

Colouring Outside the Lines

If you are anything like me, you don't like being put into a box. It's not that I don't like conforming or that I don't like being told what to do. I just like to do things my way!

I think this stems back to my days in primary school. From the very outset of our education, teachers give us pictures to colour and tell us to be careful and make sure we stay within the lines. Why? Why do we have to stay within the lines that other people have drawn? It may make a "better" picture, but it suppresses creativity! So as far back as I can remember, I have hated staying inside the lines. I hate constricting myself to boundaries set by others. Unfortunately, for years I mistook this hating to be bound by others' rules for disliking structure. While we can refuse to live within others' expectations, we need to learn to appreciate not only the importance of structures but also their God-given place. I'll try and illustrate what I mean.

I love water. Being in it, on it, around it, or under it. I also love the north coast of Northern Ireland. It is one of the most beautiful coastlines I know, and whenever possible, we as a family spend time there just walking, relaxing, going for bike rides, and chilling out. I was sitting on a beach one sunny day in May waiting to go body boarding, drinking in just how creative God is. I was watching the waves, and while I was looking at the breakers and wondering how and why God decided to put the foamy white bits on them, Genesis 1 hit me in a new way. I started to think about creation differently. The first chapter of God's revealed word is full of structure for us. When God created the sea and the sand he already had structure and process in place. Why did God create sand? Was it just for us to build sand castles and get it stuck between our toes? While both are good reasons, He created sand as part of a process and structure that He had designed.

As the waves (also part of various other processes, one that involves the gravitational pull of the moon) crash, they break down shells no longer needed by the little shellfish; together, with rock and pebbles, they all crash together, and sand is formed.

Take the time to read Genesis 1.

Now there are more than a couple of lessons to learn here.

Firstly

God created sand. He did it once. He does not appear at the seaside every night to re-create sand. He put a process in place that ensured sand would continue to be there (even if people take some of it home) without having to be constantly re-creating it. We need to ask ourselves, do we spend our life re-creating things? In our business, church or family life there are things that we do today and then will have to go back and do again tomorrow and the next day, and the next day. If we want to be effective and efficient, we have to ensure that in as many areas as possible we have self-perpetuating systems in place, where appropriate. (We also need to ensure that we don't confuse this principle with just starting something and then leaving it unmonitored!)

Sometimes our reluctance to let go of control means that we spend our time being caught up in things that could (and should) run without us.

Secondly

God was methodical in Genesis 1. He thought things out. He had a very logical process. He split up the task of creation into clearly defined steps. Each step had a measurable quantity; things were created in a progression. Fish weren't created until the water had been separated into seas. Trees had to wait until the dry land was formed. In verse 14 when God put the stars in place, they were to give us seasons, days, and years. Again He was creating structure, process, and order. He was extravagant in His planning, design, and creativity.

He stopped after each day and reviewed what He had done. He then took pleasure in what He had completed. Why did God stop every day? Was He tired? Obviously not. Did He run out of time? No. I believe that God was giving us principles at the very outset of the world.

Plan

When we set out to do something, we need to clearly think out what we are trying to achieve. When we have done that, we then need to break it down into logical, thought-out, measurable steps. Sometimes we get stressed because of our lack of forethought, and we come up against problems we could have avoided with a little more planning at the outset. We start a task by prioritising and doing the things we like to do as opposed to what we really need to be and should be doing. Maybe fish are our thing; we like fish; we're good at fish. We create our fish on day one, and then realise we aren't ready for them until day four; we've nowhere to put them and we're now behind schedule.

Focus

Even if we prioritise and plan, we still have the potential to become stressed. This can come from a lack of focus. We need to focus on the task to be done today and not be distracted by tomorrow's or the next day's task. If we don't, we might perform tasks from day one but worry about a potential problem that we may face on day five or six. This distraction can lead to losing focus and to being side tracked.

Review
At the end of each day in Genesis, God looks at what He does that day and thinks; *This was a good day's work*. We need to do that. Review. Look at what we have achieved; enjoy what we have achieved. Appreciate that we have moved forward. We have made progress. Sometimes we can be so worried by the amount of work we still have to do that it steals our joy of appreciating that we are closer to our goals than we were yesterday. We need to enjoy each stage of the task and not just push ourselves to the finish line. That's one of my major problems. I tend to focus on just the finish line. I do this at the expense of enjoying each stage. I'm tempted to see whether, if I put my mind to it and work hard, could I get creation done in five days.

God has challenged and taught me much and continues to challenge me on this!

OK, fine. Structure may work when you're God and creating the world, but can it really work in real, everyday life?

Consider another biblical man named Daniel. He was a busy man, probably busier than any of us. He was at the top in the corridors of political power in the major world power of his day. He served three different kings. Can you imagine the pressure of serving a very tetchy king, who didn't suffer fools and only wanted the right answers? Give him the wrong steer, and you ran the risk of losing your head or becoming lion food. Despite all of the risks and challenges, with God's blessing, Daniel was successful. However, Daniel's peers loathed him and his success and were out not only to end his career but also his life. This makes even today's cutthroat business world seem tame by comparison.

Against this backdrop we see a man who had structure, especially when it came to spending time with God. He prayed three times a day. He went to a set place at a set time to do a set thing. While spontaneity can be good and has its place, so too is a degree of structure. When we read Daniel 6 we find that it was through his routine and structure that Daniel's enemies would try to cause his downfall. Those who were seeking his demise knew how highly Daniel valued spending structured time with God. So much so that when these men tricked the king to issue a decree banning worship or prayer to anyone but the king, Daniel was prepared to defy the decree at the risk of a death sentence.

Now when Daniel learned that the decree had been published, he went home to his upstairs room where the windows opened toward Jerusalem. Three times a day he got down on his knees and prayed, giving thanks to his God, just as he had done before. — Daniel 6:10

No matter how busy we are, we should be taking time regularly to spend with God. He should not be an interruption to our day or tacked onto the end of our day; He should be an integral part of it, start, middle, and end.

In Genesis, God shows us that He used process and structure in creation. In the book of Daniel, we see Daniel use structure in his day-to-day political life. In the New Testament, we see Jesus use structure and process in His ministry.

How would you have dealt with a problem like the feeding of the five thousand? Have you ever been in one of those management courses where you are given all sorts of role-plays and problem solving scenarios? I have, and I'm sorry to anyone who runs them, but I hate them! But here's the ultimate problem-solving scenario: You're tired. You're emotionally drained. You've tried to head away for a bit of peace and quiet, but you still can't get away from people who want your help. They follow you. They have your mobile number and keep calling you. At this point you're probably telling them to leave you alone; you need a little "me" time. But still they need you, and you dig deep and minister even though you feel like you need ministered to yourself. Then they want you to feed them! Are you ready to shout out in exasperation, "Everyone wants a slice!"? I know I would be.

Take the time to read Mark 6.
Here we find Jesus is faced with a scenario just like this. John, his cousin, had just been beheaded by Herod. He and the disciples head off to a lonely place, and the crowd find out and follow Him. He ministers to them all day, and then they all want a BBQ!

How does Jesus feed the five thousand?
We know well that He prays to His father to bless the loaves and fishes, but then He gets practical as well. In some situations we firstly forget to ask God for His help and His blessing. Then sometimes we do, but then we forget that we have a practical part to play as well. How do you feed five thousand people? Ever had a BBQ for a church youth group? Trying to feed one hundred people when you *have* enough food is enough of a challenge.

In Mark 6, Jesus splits them into small groups of fifties and of one hundreds.

Then Jesus directed them to have all the people sit down in groups on the green grass. So they sat down in groups of hundreds and fifties. —Mark 6:39-40

How do you eat an elephant? In. Small. Bites. Take a big problem of five thousand people, and reduce it down into more manageable chunks. Sometimes we get stressed because of the size of the tasks we face, or we don't know where to start. The first step should always be, break it down into less-intimidating tasks.

After Jesus broke the crowd into smaller groups, the disciples were then each given a basket, and they distributed the food amongst the groups. Did Jesus try to do it all on his own? No. Why? Well I believe it was to show us, firstly, that if we are leaders and are supposed to deal with a lot, then we need to delegate some tasks to others while we oversee the whole process. We are not necessarily to feed everyone on our own, but rather we are to ensure that everyone is fed. Also it shows the importance of a shared task and goal. By doing this Jesus also gave the disciples worth and a ministry. At times there are things we attempt to do by ourselves, but by doing so, we are just adding to our stress and burdens, and we may be robbing others of a ministry by not asking for their assistance or not involving them.

So, systems and structure have their places, just not when it comes to colouring inside the lines!

2

Rabbit in the Headlights

It's not the mountain in your way that will stop you but the grain of sand in your shoe.
Robert W. Service

When we face huge problems, we usually react in one of two ways. We put our collars up and say, "Bring it on," or we freeze with fear, not knowing where or how to start. How we react can depend on a lot of factors. It can be based on the nature of the task or our mind-sets at the time, our physical fitness or tiredness, the time of the year, or other things that are on our plates. How we react is also related to our closeness to or distance from God.

In those times when we put our collars up, we don't usually feel stressed; we just get on with the jobs at hand. It's the times when we stare at a task and can't do anything that stress us and hinder us from making progress. Those situations intimidate us. They cause a shadow to fall over all areas of our lives.

The Israelites faced the same problem. They lived in the shadow of a giant problem, and his name was Goliath!

Take the time to read 1 Samuel 17. Here we read how every morning and every evening Goliath came and taunted them. He belittled them. He made them live in fear and with a feeling of helplessness. He told them, "You don't know how to handle me; you can't handle me. You have to live under the shadow of me, and life can't move on." No one knew what to do about Goliath. The king didn't even know.

Do you have a problem like that? It's with you in the morning when you wake up. It's still undealt with when you go to bed. It taunts you because you just don't know what to do or where to start.

Let's go back to our story in 1 Samuel 17 to learn how to confront a giant. David comes to deliver cheese to his brothers. He sees the problem. He doesn't focus on the size and enormity of it. He just sees a problem that needs dealt with before life can move on. He sees that to leave this problem unresolved is at odds with God's plan, and that it is a mockery of God and His power to let it triumph.

The king provides David with armour to help him, but it hinders him. Sometimes that happens to us. Others can be well meaning and give us advice of what we should and shouldn't do. Sometimes that can be helpful, but be careful, as what works for someone else might not work for you. We can try to get complex ways to deal with our situation, but this can add to the stress, not relieve it. Whatever we do, we should never try to fight our battles using someone else's armour, but more on that later!

David keeps it simple with five stones, one sling, and Goliath's soft, exposed forehead. He assessed his problem, and he took practical steps to then confront it...with God's blessing. David hit Goliath in the head, and Goliath crashed to the ground—where he was a lot easier to deal with. Once he was on the ground, David finished the job off. It's also worthy of remembering that on that day, under pressure of all the Israelites, Philistines, and Goliath watching, David was able to use his sling with confidence as he had spent many days in private practising and perfecting his skill. That's a different point that we'll look at in a few pages, but to be able to "perform" in public, we need to have spent many hours practicing in private!

We need to look at our own giants. There are areas to start with. We need to focus on details and not just see the whole, big problem. We need to accurately assess them, and then make a plan of attack, a plan of where we will start. When we face our giants, we need to make a plan of attack, go and get our stones, and then make a start. Again I must stress this. We must make a start! Even the longest journey starts with a single step. We can get intimidated with how much we need to do. It's a natural reaction. Sometimes we don't even realise it, as it happens subconsciously. It comes over us like a dark cloud.

We pray about it; we really seek God's face, but nothing seems to happen. Does God not hear us? Does He not understand how it is making us feel?

God equips us to deal with things, but He expects us to do our bit.

Take time to read Joshua 7. Here we read of the children of Israel going into battle against Ai. They get routed. They are shocked. They have no idea how they will deal with not only the defeat but how they will regroup and go into battle against Ai once again. Joshua does what we would consider to be a good thing, and it is. He goes to his tent, and he prays. He brings his problem to God in prayer.

What does God do?

The LORD said to Joshua, "Stand up! What are you doing down on your face? Israel has sinned; they have violated my covenant, which I commanded them to keep. They have taken some of the devoted things; they have stolen, they have lied, they have put them with their own possessions. That is why the Israelites cannot stand against their enemies; they turn their backs and run because they have been made liable to destruction. I will not be with you anymore unless you destroy whatever among you is devoted to destruction." —Joshua 7:10–12

God tells Joshua to stop praying and to get up and do something. There was sin in the camp. It needed dealt with. He basically told Joshua, "You know what to do. Go do it." There is a time to pray. There is a time to act. Sometimes we don't take things to God in prayer. Sometimes we pray and expect things to happen, but God would have us take action and do what we know we need to do. There's no point in leaning on a shovel and praying that God will send you a hole!

When we take action and strike down our giants, we grow. We grow because we are victorious and, having been taunted, we have proved that through God's help, we can do it. David took five stones from the brook. He used one for Goliath. He had four left. Goliath had four brothers. I get a picture that David not only dealt with the immediate giant but was ready for the next four if they came to taunt him.

Way back when Moses sent spies into the Promised Land to see what it was like, they came back and said that there were giants in the land. Two of the spies said, "Let's go; with God's help we can take them." The remaining ten were intimidated and said, "They are too great for us." Because of that mind-set and because of the reluctance to deal with those giants, the children of Israel spent forty years wandering in the desert marking time, not moving forward and not enjoying the land that God had promised.

We have a choice. We can remain intimidated by the giant problems. We can bottle the need to do something, to dig deep, to take action and instead choose to live our lives stressed by the taunting and intimidation of our problems, not living in the promises of God. Or, we can take action.

Make a start. Look for ways of breaking the problem down so it's easier to deal with. We can then move forward and be victorious in life.

3

Have You a Watch but No Time?

Do you spend time or invest it?

Over the past few years, I've been blessed to be able to work alongside a charity that builds schools in East Africa. Starting as a "small" dream to buy and work a teaching farm in Uganda, the work of Fields of Life has been blessed and has grown almost beyond belief, building over one hundred schools in less than fifteen years in East Africa. As I write this, I'm privileged to be in Uganda, sitting in a hut with a banana leaf roof, looking out over Lake Victoria with the mist rising in the distance. While I've been here, I've thought a lot about time.

Here, they say to me, "You have a watch and no time; I have no watch and plenty of time!" It pains me to know that they're right.

Back in the western world, we say that time is money, and in a sense, it is. In any business, wages are one of, if not the largest, overheads; but here in Africa, man-hours are cheap. Instead of saying "time is money," I think it might be truer to say "time or money", you can have one or the other but not both. In the West, most of us have money, but we complain we don't have time. It's not a new thing. There's a song by the Eagles that says, "You can spend all your time making money, you can spend all your money making time." Here in Uganda people have little or no money, but they have a lot of time.

Time is Precious

Time is probably the most precious resource we have. In life we all have been given different abilities and gifts, but we all receive the same amount of time every day.

Jesus told two stories about servants receiving talents and how they used them.

Take time to read both in Matthew 25 and Luke 19.

In Matthew 25:15, the master gives different amounts of talents, or coins, to the different servants. One of the lessons we can learn from this is that while we may have different gifts, money, and resources than others, the master is interested in what we do with what *we* have been given.

The other parable in Luke 19:12 speaks of a different situation where all the servants receive talents equally. I believe this can be applied to our time. No matter who we are, we all are given twenty-four hours in a day—whether we are rich or poor or we live in Africa or America. It is our most precious resource, as we *have* to spend it. We can't store it, save it, bank it, build it up, or leave it to our kids. Once it's gone, it's gone. We can, however, invest it! One of the applications from the parable in Luke is that we need to invest wisely to please our master.

How do you invest yours?

Ever said, "There're just not enough hours in the day," or "There're not enough days in the week!"? I have. And it's wrong. There are enough; it's just how we choose to use them.

As we've already seen, when God created the world, it tells us in Genesis 1 that He ordained times, days, and seasons. He caused all the planets to spin in orbits to provide us with a day that would last for twenty-four hours. When He laid out creation, He ordained a seven-day week, with a built-in rest day. When I say there aren't enough hours in the day or enough days in the week, without even realising it, I've said that God got it wrong! Obviously He didn't. So, if He got it right, and He did, and I don't have enough time to do everything, I must be filling my 24/7 with things I don't need to do. So, I need to be structured in how I use this precious resource.

When we spend our money, we spend it first on the most important things, the essentials (or at least we should). We tithe, we pay the mortgage, we pay food bills, and we pay utility bills. Then we spend our disposable income.

What about our time?

Dorothy Canfield Fisher said, "If we only gave the same amount of reflection to what we want out of life as we give to what to do with two-weeks' vacation, we would be startled at our false standards and the aimless procession of our busy days."
Does that strike a nerve?

What is the most important thing we can spend our time on? Jesus, while on Earth, was busy. There were so many demands on his time by so many people, but He was able to say in John 6:38,
For I have come down from heaven not to do my own will, but the will of him who sent me.

We have prioritised to do our Father's will first. For me, I spend a lot of time doing things that aren't my Father's will, and that's the problem. We need to establish what God's primary purpose for our lives are, and then fit the other things in.

Jesus touched, impacted, and changed so many lives, and there was always someone wanting his time, but He needed to spend time Himself, with God. Jesus needed to spend time with His Father God, "in stillness and quietness," to ensure that He did the will of his Father. It was alone in the garden of Gethsemane that He prayed, "Not my will but yours," not only establishing His Father's will, but also submitting to His Father's will. If God's own son needed to do this, how much more do we?

Jesus was so protective of His time and priorities that even when a close friend was ill and subsequently died, He still didn't change His schedule. However, we need to be careful not to mistake the account in chapter 11 of John's gospel as showing Jesus as uncaring and inflexible; rather, we need to understand it in light of His vision and focus. Jesus obviously did care, as we read further in the story, one of the most beautiful verses in the Bible, a verse that shows His love, His humanity, His empathy, and so many things. John 11:35, *Jesus wept.* He didn't change plans and go rushing to Lazarus because He understood God's will, purpose, and timing.

In Mark 5:21–24, Jairus came to Jesus, wanting him to come to his house to heal his daughter. As Jesus accompanied Jairus, a crowd of people wanted His attention. In the midst of wanting to go to this little girl, in the midst of the crowd, Jesus was still able to take time to be aware of those around Him and was able to help someone who needed His touch. He then went and helped the little girl. He knew when to act and when to wait. We can be too reactive to our diaries, and while there are times that we need to be, there are occasions when we need to say no, be strong, and remember that no one can take our time; it is ours alone to give.

4

If You Want a Haircut, Go Yourself...

My father has a lot of sayings, but one of his favourites is, "If you want a haircut, go yourself!" He was basically giving the advice that if you want something done, do it yourself. Sometimes this is very good advice, but not all the time.

It can be so much easier to do things ourselves. After all, *we're* good at it. We can do it quickly. We don't want to waste time showing others; by the time we'd show someone else how to do it, we would have it done.

But it's not always about us. It's not always just about getting the job done; it can be about what is achieved during the task, not just getting the task done.

An old proverb says, "It is better to journey than to arrive," but in our busy lives, sometimes we are so focused on the destination that we lose the joy and beauty of our journey. Flying from New York to LA is certainly quicker, but I'm sure driving there along Route 66 would leave you with a lot more memories, sights, and sounds!

A good friend of mine, who is quite well off financially, once shared a heartfelt lesson he had learnt. He is a man who is more in tune with God than most people I know. Part of God's calling on his life is communicating. One evening after a speaking engagement, he was approached by a lady who told him that she wanted to bless him financially by giving him a cheque for £100. He told her kindly not to worry about it, because God had provided for him financially by other means, and he didn't need additional support. She pressed him, as she felt that she had been prompted to give him this amount, but again he refused, as God had more than adequately provided for his material needs from other sources. He left without accepting her cheque. Later that evening he realised to his great regret that what was happening was that God was working in this lady, and it wasn't about him. He had, through his pride, stolen her opportunity to bless; he had taken her opportunity to be obedient to God's prompting and had taken away her opportunity of service that evening. While most of us would never think of refusing £100, we do in many other ways hinder or steal people's service. To add insult to injury, not only do we steal the service of others, but we do it and add to our time pressures and stress. So why do it?

Part of it is pride. No one can do that job just as good as me. I do it well. If I want it done to the best standard, I need to do it myself. This can give us a sense of worth and a feeling of being needed.

Part of it is practical. It's quicker. We're busy people. We hardly have time to do the task ourselves, let alone take twice the time to show someone how to do it.

Part of it can be control. We like to do some tasks because by keeping them for ourselves, it gives us power; it gives us control.

I'm Irish, so I can tell this story. Paddy and Mick were in the jungle when suddenly, from behind a clump of grass, leaps a ferocious lion. Paddy immediately takes his rucksack off his back, opens it, takes out his running shoes, and puts them on. Mick looks at him in disbelief and says, "Sure, Paddy, what are ye doing? You'll never outrun that lion!"

"I know," replies Paddy, "but I don't need to outrun the lion, I just need to outrun you!"

Sometimes that's our attitude. We are concerned about being just a little better than those around us. A little smarter, a little more responsible, just a little more. While outrunning Mick is good in the short-term for Paddy, it's definitely not good for Mick. It is like that too for those around us if we try to just do things that are only right for us.

Early in my leadership roles, I was told that a good leader is one who makes him or herself redundant. However, some people lead by keeping everything to themselves, not letting those who follow them in on what's going on, not involving them or giving them tasks to do. This is counterproductive. What it does is disempower people. Without realising it, people can't make a decision without your input. They can't complete a task without you. Everyone needs you to be able to function. This means they need you, and that makes you feel good. It also means they all want and need a slice of your time, and that makes you feel stressed.

That's why it's important to delegate. (It's also important as a leader to know when and what *not* to share!) But while you can delegate authority, you can't delegate responsibility!

What do I mean? While you can delegate tasks, ultimately it is still your responsibility to ensure that they are done and done well. That means it is important to be there for people. It is important that you're not just giving out all the tasks and not doing anything yourself. It's important that you make sure people aren't feeling inadequate or unsupported or untrained.

Take the time now to read Exodus 18.

In this passage we are given an insight into delegation. Moses led the children of Israel. He started by leading them out of Egypt, and through time he got used to doing the leading thing all by himself. It can happen to us. We don't all start off wanting to do it ourselves, but that's the way it can end up, either because of the reasons stated above, or through people letting us down. Moses was doing it all himself and burning out, but he was so engrossed as a leader, he didn't even realise. He didn't know what to do to change it. He was given some advice from his family. Family are good people to give us advice. They see how things are behind the scenes when we're not at the front, when we're not playing the role expected of us. His father-in-law came to him and told him to get a grip. He basically said, "Yes, you can do it; yes, you have been doing it, but you will burn out, and then you're no use to anyone."

Moses' father-in-law replied, "What you are doing is not good. You and these people who come to you will only wear yourselves out. The work is too heavy for you; you cannot handle it alone." —Exodus 18:17–18

As a young person I remember hearing it preached that it is, "Good to burn out for God," and, "Better to burn out than rust out!" It seems very noble and romantic, but ultimately I don't believe it is God's way.

Thankfully, Moses wasn't too proud to heed his father-in-law's advice. Acting on this older man's wisdom and insight, he put in place a leadership structure. He chose people of character and responsibility. He then empowered them to do what he needed them to do. Moses also let the children of Israel know of the changes, so they wouldn't be left confused and wondering who they should go to when they needed help.

I'm sure there were people who wanted to speak directly to Moses because they'd always spoken to him. There will always be people who want to bypass the structures we put in place (and there are always exceptions to every rule), but for us to be able to cope with our tasks, we need to keep them structured.

First go to the leader of the fifty. If it's still not sorted, go to the leader of the one hundred. If it's still not sorted, go to the leader of the one thousand. By doing this, Moses was freed up from the smaller problems (while still important and still needing addressed), which could be dealt with by others, and he was able to spend time with God and get on with the overall strategic leadership that God had given him to do. He was able to do the bit that God wanted him to do and wasn't distracted from his task.

So how do we apply that to ourselves? Well, what are the things that we are doing that, while needing done, could and probably should be done by others? God has gifted us all in different ways. What might be a drag and drudgery to you may be a blessed area of service for another. While you continue to do it, you eat into your time and don't have enough time or focus to do what is your calling, and you may be, without realising it, stealing their areas of blessing.

5

Seashells and Shades

On a business trip to America, I found myself unable to sleep early one morning. We'd arrived the previous night in the pitch dark, but I knew the hotel we were staying in was beside the ocean. After passing two hours of restlessness trying to sleep, I thought I might as well get up and go for a walk and see the sunrise.

Wow. It was beautiful. The sea or the scenery hadn't changed from the previous night; it was just now that I could see it. It had been there the whole time, but that's a different lesson!

As it was January, it was cold, about minus ten, with clear skies as I walked along the beach. Part of why I couldn't sleep was the jet lag, part was a busy mind concerned with the upcoming business meetings. Would this trip be successful? Would I crash and burn? As I walked, I prayed, and God drew close. As I've already said, I love being near the sea, and as I walked I studied the shells and driftwood strewn across the beach. I stopped and gazed out to sea. When I looked down, something caught my eye. When I looked closer, it was a pair of sunglasses that had obviously been dropped and

washed out at sea. But on the glasses were tiny barnacles. These little shellfish had made these sunglasses their home.

Barnacles do that. They make their home on whatever they can, no complaining about what they have or haven't, what they need, or what they could do if they just had better resources. They just use whatever God has provided for them at that moment. These barnacles, God was telling me, made the best of whatever they had with no complaints.

If you are like most people, we quite often think that we could do more or better if circumstances were just a bit different. We can convince ourselves that it is easier for others.

We can feel under pressure because of a lack of confidence in ourselves, in our gifts, and our abilities. We can look at others and see them as more gifted, more confident with more going for them. Do you find yourself in a situation where you feel overwhelmed and out of your depth?

Moses struggled too. At the age of forty he had believed he was to deliver the Israelites and attempted to do so when he was "properly" equipped as part of

Pharaoh's house in a position of power and influence. However that wasn't the right time and it didn't work out well. When he encounters God in the desert forty years later, he's full of excuses. Before we get too hard on Moses, consider how we would have reacted. If you've ever left a job to go back to the same office a few years later, you'll know that things have moved on, and while there will be some people who will remember you, many won't, and they definitely wouldn't take any instructions from you. Having spent forty years in the back of the desert looking after sheep, I'm sure Moses's years in the palace seemed like they came from a different life. I'm sure Moses was genuine in how he felt, and he started to try and reason God out of his logic, but God was having none of it.

Take the time to read Exodus 4.

Moses asks God why people would take him seriously, what he could do or what he has that would make him successful in his mission. God responds with a simple, "What have you got in your hand?" He makes Moses start by looking and thinking about what he has, no matter how insignificant it may seem. He had his staff. He had probably gotten so used to using it every day that he took it for granted.

What is your staff? Is there something that God has given you that you use every day, but you have become so accustomed to that you no longer consider it useful beyond what you currently do with it? Just as Moses's staff was useful, when used as God commanded, it became alive. Do you need God to transform what is in your hand?

Even though Moses was afraid of the serpent that God turned his staff into, God showed him not to fear. The snake that was dangerous and potentially harmful was harmless to Moses because he acted as God commanded. But what if he had lost his staff? Well, God covered that too. He told Moses to put his hand inside his cloak, and when he took it out again, it was diseased. He put it in again and it was healed. God made his body; He could smite him or heal him. God illustrated that He is able to show His power even though we might not have anything we think of value. God took the sick, diseased hand and healed it.

He wants to take broken and ill hands and heal them to be used for His purposes and glory. Do you feel broken; do you feel ill? Trust God, and He will take you as you are, change you, and He will empower you.

It's not only a case of using what's in your hand, but you also need to use it in a way that is suited you.

I have already mentioned how David had been sent to deliver some cheese and bread to his brothers. When he arrived at the army camp, he couldn't believe his eyes and ears. God's people were standing by, letting a giant called Goliath ridicule and mock them and God. Simple faith made David step forward to take on the giant. When the king and his advisors heard about this and started to prepare David, they tried to help by offering him and dressing him in the king's armour. Remember that when Saul was made king, he was described as being a head taller than any other person, so while his armour would have been the best gear, I'm sure it was heavy and huge on David. Fortunately, David was not afraid to speak out to these experienced men, and he said to them that he couldn't possibly wear the armour, as he wasn't used to it. Instead, he took what was in his hand, his sling, went to the river, took five stones, and then he went to fight. He wasn't prepared to fight wearing another man's armour.

Then Saul dressed David in his own tunic. He put a coat of armour on him and a bronze helmet on his head. David fastened on his sword over the tunic and tried walking around, because he was not used to them. "I cannot go in these," he said to Saul, "because I am not used to them." So he took them off. Then he took his staff in his hand, chose five smooth stones from the stream, put them in the pouch of his shepherd's bag and, with his sling in his hand, approached the Philistine.
—1 Samuel 17:38–40

Have you ever tried to do that? Today, it mightn't be their armour; it might be their style, their manner, or some other way. One of the reasons God wants us to use what is in our hands is that He wants us to be ourselves. If we try to do things the way someone else does, like David, we will be awkward and untested. God wants you to use things in the way only you can. That's why He created you and called you.

Now we also have a responsibility to hone and refine what He gave us. Paul talks to Timothy in 2 Timothy 1:6 about fanning gifts into flame.

For this reason I remind you to fan into flame the gift of God, which is in you through the laying on of my hands. —2 Timothy 1:6

Proverbs 27:16 tells us to seek others to help us do that. As iron sharpening iron is how one person should sharpen another.

David didn't just go on a whim; read the passage. He speaks of how he had practised with his sling in the fields on his own when he was looking after sheep. While he practiced, sometimes the target changed from a tree stump to a bear or a lion. He needed not just to be accurate, but when the bear or lion came, he also had to be brave and accurate under pressure! David was able to be victorious in the public battlefield because of his faith in God and his preparation in the private place. That seems to be largely at odds with a lot of thinking today. Many seek acclaim and the public stage but aren't prepared for the unseen private preparation.

If a middle-aged "has-been" shepherd who had been hiding in the desert for forty years could lead over one million people, and if a trainee shepherd who delivered groceries could defeat giants and become king, what do you think God could do with you if you trust Him and use what He's given you?

6

Love Many, Trust Few, Always Paddle Your Own Canoe...

Sailors. Used to the sea. Used to hard rowing. Used to frightening situations. Used to dealing with difficult stuff. One evening they set sail, same as always. It's pleasant enough. But there's no hint of what is to come. It gets dark. It gets choppy. It gets scary. They get stuck and deal with it. They dig deep and row. Things don't get any better. It turns out it's all someone else's fault. But they don't shirk responsibility; they'll get through it. All they need to do is row harder, for longer.

Take time to read Jonah 1.

As you read the story of Jonah, you find that the sailors on the ship that Jonah boarded were more interested in helping others than he was. Not only did they give him the benefit of their blood, sweat, and tears, but in trying to bring the boat and Jonah safely back to shore, it cost them financially as they had to throw their cargo over the side.

Now, there are probably times in life when you feel like Jonah, running away from what you are supposed to do, but have you ever felt like one of the sailors?

Situations, problems, or storms arise in other people's lives, and you try to help them. You invest valuable time, effort, and even money as you try to help. You do this, and all that seems to happen is while you're giving your best, they are getting nowhere. You try to row your Jonah ashore because you'll be there for him, and you'll see him through it. What if it's not God's will that you row them ashore?

For many years as a youth leader, I tried so hard with so many of our young people to help them through their storms. Sometimes the storms were like the ones in Mark 8, in which the purpose was to show God's glory and to instil greater trust. Looking back, I believe a lot were Jonah storms—storms to deal with wrong directions, wrong choices, and deliberate disobedience. I think I have spent a lot of time and energy trying to row my Jonahs ashore. I felt it was my duty to be there for the young people regardless. Let me say that I believe (and hope) that I was always there when they needed me, but there is a point—and it isn't a point that is easily reached or reached without a lot of prayerful thought and soul-searching, but there is a point—where you say, I'm letting you go; I'm throwing you overboard; it is between you and God. I can't help you; you need to sort yourself out. If I just keep trying for you, all that will happen is that I *will* get stressed out and tired, and you still *won't have* dealt with the issue.

Many nights I have struggled to sleep, because I'm worried and concerned about a person in a particular situation, and do you know what? They have been fast asleep, not as concerned about it as I am. I'm wrecking myself carrying someone else's burden.

Please, please don't mistake this as teaching people just to look out for themselves. Do all you can for people, but do not try to solve their situations when God wants to deal with them and they are resisting.

We read in Acts 2:42:

They devoted themselves to the apostles' teaching and to fellowship, to the breaking of bread and to prayer.

It says they devoted themselves to the apostles' teaching. It says they devoted *themselves*!

The situation I'm talking about is when we carry the burden of devoting people on their behalf. How much time do we spend devoting to others? I know that I've spent too much time devoting on others' behalf, always reminding them to come to church and to come out at 8:30 p.m. to the youth meeting.

As I've already said, I was more concerned about them and their situations than they were about themselves. I spent more time trying to "devote" rather than trying to lead and to guide. I wish I'd spent longer doing the latter. I don't think I'm alone in that regard; how many of you have done the same? Ask most people involved in ministry, and if they are honest, they will tell you that they've probably spent too much time trying to row Jonahs and devote them.

Now we also need to be mindful that there is a difference between helping those who *can't* help themselves and helping those who *won't* help themselves. Let me give you an example.

Take the time to read Genesis 14.

Here we read of Abram's nephew, Lot, being captured and taken away as a prisoner. Lot had chosen to live close to Sodom, and as we read the early part of Genesis 14, we see that by that choice, he had chosen to live in a very politically unstable area. He placed himself in a dangerous situation, and things didn't work out well. It could have been easy for Abram to look and think that Lot was in his situation because of his own poor choices and decisions, and that he got what was coming to him. He might have justifiably felt that he had already been more than generous to Lot by letting him choose where he would live first, and that he owed Lot nothing. But without hesitation, Abram gets together a small army, and at a cost and risk to himself, goes to liberate his nephew. He is quickly successful, and Lot is freed. This story illustrates to us that we should, when we are prompted of God, give ourselves to help those in genuine need and who are unable to help themselves.

However, we need to have much wisdom and discernment in being careful to distinguish those who can't help themselves from those who just won't help themselves but are happy to sit back and let us use *our* energy and efforts on them. If we fail to recognise the difference, we may end up trying to row our Jonahs and fall into the trap of being busy but not productive. Our time and energy is sapped by tasks that get us and those around us no further forward, but not only that, they keep us from doing what we should be doing.

Jesus spoke in Matthew 11:28–30 about an easy yoke.

Come to me, all you who are weary and burdened, and I will give you rest. Take my yoke upon you and learn from me, for I am gentle and humble in heart, and you will find rest for your souls. For my yoke is easy and my burden is light.

If we feel that we are burdened and under a heavy yoke, we need to ask ourselves whose yoke we are in; it can't be God's, so who does it belong to and why are we under it?

Now, again, I must stress to you, please, please understand that I'm not trying to encourage you to just look out for yourself, because that's not God's way either. In Galatians 6:2–5 Paul tells us to carry each other's burdens.

Carry each other's burdens, and in this way you will fulfil the law of Christ. If anyone thinks they are something when they are not, they deceive themselves. Each one should test their own actions. Then they can take pride in themselves alone, without comparing themselves to someone else, for each one should carry their own load.

While we are to help carry others' burdens, Paul means it is a sharing of that burden with our brother or sister; he's not telling us to take it off them. It is the idea of working together in partnership in which everyone is pulling their weight. This is perfectly illustrated in Exodus 17 by Moses, Arran, and Hur.

While Joshua led the children of Israel into battle against the Amalekites, Moses went with Arran and Hur to a hill that overlooked the battle. While Moses had his hands raised, the Israelites prevailed, but when his arms grew weary, the Israelites started to lose the battle. Now Moses was an experienced leader. Moses was a mighty man of God. Moses had stood before Pharaoh, but Moses was a man, who in the midst of vital leadership tasks, became weary and worn out.

But Moses had men with him who would help him—men who would share his burden and help him through the task at hand. These men stood at either side and took hold of his hands, raised them above his head, and helped him to hold them. They helped Moses as they saw him trying, giving his best but unable to do it on his own. The effort and energy of Arran and Hur was well spent, as through their support, Moses endured, and the children of Israel won their battle.

I believe this shows the pattern of sharing each other's burdens by combining our energy and efforts with those who are giving of theirs.
If we don't want to end up tired, weary, and achieving little, we need to make sure that those we are working with and helping are interested in helping themselves and prepared to put in some of the effort! If you don't want to become unnecessarily weary and worn out, be careful not to take on an unequal yoke!

Preview

Coming soon.......

ALL DISHED
OUT......
Living when you've nothing left.

Johnnie Black

Made in the USA
Charleston, SC
10 December 2014